Italian Women
and
Other Tragedies

To Mel
in the to
struggle to
communicate
love
Gianna
Patriarca

Essential Poets Series 62

Gianna Patriarca

Italian Women and Other Tragedies

Guernica
Toronto / New York
1996

Antonio D'Alfonso, editor.
Guernica Editions Inc.
P. O. Box 117, Station P, Toronto (ON), Canada M5S 2S6
340 Nagel Drive, Cheektowaga, N.Y. 14225-4731 U.S.A.

The publisher acknowledges the support of The Canada Council
and The Ontario Arts Council.

Second Printing.

Legal Deposit — Second Quarter
National Library of Canada.
Library of Congress Catalog Card Number: 93-73686.

Canadian Cataloguing in Publication Data
Patriarca, Gianna
Italian Women and other tragedies
(Essential poets ; 62)
ISBN 1-55071-001-X
I. Title. II. Series.
PS8581. A78398183 1994 C811'.54 C93-090575-X
PS9199.3.P38183 1994

Table of Contents

These poems are for my mother, Antonietta
and in memory of my father, Luciano

and always for Andrew and Gia

Italian Women

these are the women
who were born to give birth

they breathe only
leftover air
and speak only
when deeper voices
have fallen asleep

i have seen them bleed
in the dark
hiding the stains inside them
like sins
apologizing

i have seen them wrap their souls
around their children
and serve their own hearts
in a meal they never
share.

My Birth

my father is a great martyr
he has forgiven me everything
even my female birth.

January was a bitch of a month
when i raised my head, for the
first time
from my mother's stained and
aching womb

a dozen relatives waited in the kitchen
to see the prize in the easter egg

how i disappointed them
my father's first child
was not male

i swear i can still hear the
only welcoming sounds
were from my mother
and she has always been blamed
for the mistake

for weeks
my father was drunk on red wine
mourning the loss of his own
immortality

Daughters

my father called me whore
and my mother cried

a young Italian woman's
claim to prostitution
is any activity past
the midnight hour

his eyes were coral
as he rammed his fist
inside my mouth
reminding me

and my mother screamed

the walls are knocking
how will they face the
neighbours in the morning

if only i could be more
like my married sister
or the virgin daughters
of the virgin neighbours

and how did the Devil
come to live inside our house?

and my mother prays

Paesaggi

she waved her dark hand
by the open gate
in a town that grew
like a mole from the
side of a hill

her face was the shade
of fine white marble

he held the suitcase
secured
by the leather belt
and his steps left no prints
on the sun bleached pebbles

thirteen days
the ocean was endless

the waves were the shade
of fine white marble

the days, the weeks
the months grew
like children

for a thousand seasons
she stood by the gate
in the morning
in the evening
when the rain came

from the ocean into silence
all the years were
her grandchildren.

Maggio

gli alberi
hanno finalmente
deciso
di ridere

come mia mamma rideva
prima del cambio
della nuova terra

prima di svegliarsi
accanto
allo scuro estraneo

prima di riconoscere
che mia sorella
non voleva più
fiocchi

questo mese
i fiori appaiano
belli

questo mese
scanzerò tutto
sono ubriaca
di alberi

May

the trees
have finally decided
to laugh

the way my mother laughed
before the changes
the new country

before she woke up to
the dark stranger
in her bed

before she recognized
my sister didn't care
for ribbons

this month the
flowers appear most
beautiful

this month i can put
aside anything
i am drunk with trees

Contrasti

i am not the fine
white, English flesh
that holds those eyes
the ones who borrowed
the clearest blue from
a Pacific island sky.

i have not the small
gentle hands
you mistook for wild flowers
and photographed endlessly
in gardens
orchards
in sleepy city lofts

i am not the one
whose hair ignites
sun-fire in afternoons

i come to you
from peasant stock
from gardens of large rocks
where thirsty flowers
lie unphotographed

Conversations

for Lucy

there is that much love
mysterious
your eyes, opening
emptying like fountains in European summers
words flow between us
stopping at the heart
while, outside, the wind bites into March

three a.m.
and the sleep goes out for recess
the way the children will tomorrow
and you and i
will be making motions
trying to make sense of the night before
why it seemed so important
the words
the cigarettes
the espresso
him

i sometimes wonder
where we will be years from now
were we there already?
alone,
together
at different times
the questions happen often
usually at three a.m.
when i can't sleep
and i remember your eyes.

For Roberto Pisapia

(Resident of Villa Colombo*)

you sit
flesh like stone
one leg less
a neighbour of death
your eyes draped by cataracts
they see me
but don't recognize
the face you smiled at
for years, across a small table
in the neighbourhood café

Roberto, how quickly
time gives a final embrace

last July we laughed
talked of your days of song
with Caruso
the climbing lights on the head of Vesuvius
the streets of Naples flirting in the night

it is a long way from Naples
to Villa Colombo

here, they have built you a fountain
they place your wheelchair by its
ceramic border
i know your ears are fighting
its fraudulent sound

Roberto, we will not speak again
until our eyes
are the stars over the
Bay of Naples.

* Villa Colombo is an Old Age Residence

Perhaps

perhaps my father would love
the colours of the olive trees
in the summer

perhaps he would stop by
the slouching, lazy leaves
of the fig tree, close his eyes
to remember the dark haired
children climbing towards the sun

perhaps he would recognize the sound
of rain on clay rooftops
or of a rooster waking the dawn

perhaps if he walked that
road of white pebbles
and reached the farmhouse
in the distance
he would touch the heads
of the newborn chicks
and recall the wonder

but for thirty years now
he's slept in a foreign bed
that has curved his spine

the corn husks of his young bed
have rotted in a cradle

if he could return
to smell the earth
his father left him
he would understand

Returning

we don't discuss the distance anymore
returning is now
the other dream
not American at all
not Canadian or Italian
it has lost its nationality.

in the sixties we came in swarms
like summer bees
smelling of something strange
wearing the last moist kiss
of our own sky.
we came with heavy trunks
empty pockets
and a dream.

i was one of them
tucked away below the sea line
on the bottom floor of a ship
that swelled and ached
for thirteen days
our bellies emptied into the Atlantic
until the ship finally vomited
on the shores of Halifax
there, where the arms and legs
of my doll fell apart into the sea
finding their way back over the waves.

my mother's young heart wrapped around me
my sister crying for bread and mortadella.
we held on
two more nights on a stiff, cold train
headed for Toronto
where the open arms of a half forgotten man
waited.

Summers with Arduino

the hills in the distance
still echo the songs you
taught them
red, revolutionary songs
and above your head
the birds
were an army in chorus.

here
the summers will never
be the same
my childhood brother
my friend.

twenty years of a
strange silence
i return
my breasts full
your hands strong
and so much time to make up
in words
in walks
through the fields
where our ancestors
planted everything with
the seed of their bones
where their spirits

still wave the bright
handkerchiefs
that saved their sweat.

i leave
i return
with the need
of your song
still searching
for similar hills
in a distant country.

Reasons

it really doesn't matter now
the reasons we left the fields
in all those towns cradled in
the gentle arms of green hills

the reasons we left the stone houses
we laughed in during the cold winters
where God was a fireplace

the reasons we left the hot summers
when finding water was a miracle
and we thanked the saints
and we thanked the priests
and we lit the candles

and when the bells sounded on Sunday mornings
we walked miles to thank the mass

it really doesn't matter now
if no one brings flowers to grandpa's grave
he never cared much for flowers anyway

and it won't matter if after you're gone
i won't remember your pain

you have always said that i'm insensitive.

i am part of this city now
the one that gives less than a damn
about our reasons.

Life is a Glass of Wine

we sit together each night
our bellies full
our legs heavy
and a glass of red wine
my uncle's best
poured into the same glasses
she had saved in the trunk
that crossed the Atlantic
with her
my sister
and me.

they were meant to be mine
in my new home
drinking my new name

that dream for another lifetime.

so, we drink the wine
in Autumn we roast the chestnuts
i listen to her delicate lips
speaking of the Roman sky
how it warmed her.

if you listen closely to the glass
you can hear the sound crickets make
in the heat of night.

Napoli 1960

un cielo di
fazzoletti bianchi
baci attraverso
un mare
una nave circola
il sole
un filo di voce
che prega
una mano di bimba
si stende
per afferrare
l'aria che
conosce

College Street, Toronto

I have come back to this street
to begin a new chapter of my inheritance
my Canadian odyssey.

for my father it began in 1956
in the basement of a Euclid Street
rooming house
with five other men
homeless, immigrant dreamers
bordanti
young, dark
handsome and strong
bricklayers
carpenters
gamblers.

they cooked their pasta
by the light of a forty watt bulb
drank bad red wine
as they argued the politics of
the country they left behind
avoiding always the new politics.
late in the evenings they
spent their loose change
in the Gatto Nero, the Bar Italia
pool, espresso
cards and cigarettes.

while in all the towns
from Friuli to Sicily
postponed families waited
for the letters, the dollars
the invitation.

then the exodus
of wives and children
trunks and wine glasses
hand stitched linens in hope chests
floating across the Atlantic
slowly
to Halifax
To Union Station
To College Street.

1960
my sister and I
cold and frightened
pushed toward a crowded gate
into the arms
of a strange man
who smelled of tobacco.

Crawford Street
three small rooms
in a three storey house
dark and airless
smelling of boiled fish.
Rose and Louis Yutzman
lived downstairs

Louis died in the middle
of a frozen January night
Rose's screams were nails
driven hard into my eardrums.

my fearless mother
touched his silent face
held his limp, large hand
as she closed his eyes
while my father and I
barefoot and trembling
hid petrified
behind the door

we learned the language quickly
to everyone's surprise
my mother embraced her new life
in long factory lines
while my father continued his pleasures
in pool halls thick with voices
of other men in exile.

1981
the Italians are almost all gone
to new neighbourhoods
modern towns.

my father is gone
Bar Italia has a new clientele
women come here now
I come here
I drink espresso and smoke cigarettes

from the large window
that swims in sunlight
I think I see my father
leaning on the parking meter
passionately arguing
the soccer scores.

How strange this city
sometimes
it seems so much smaller
than all those towns
we came from.

The Garden

New Zealand gardens
are perfect
like the people
perfectly blonde
perfectly tall
perfectly gentle

it is in these gardens
my husband took shape
beneath this Pacific sun
that does not kill
the way the Italian sun
killed my ancestors
slowly

here the ground is always alive
with roses and gum trees
that echo with magpies
but i remember rocks
large ones
my grandfather moved them
continually
and they always grew again.

i lie here
among the wild agapanthus
beneath the red Pohutakawas
how did i come so far

from Lazio
to the bottom of the world
with a tall, light man
who smells of the sea

i am the dark rose
transplanted in this
island of the long white cloud.

Pablo and You

i am alone in this room
without doors
alone with Pablo and you

his book
fat with images
of the thousand wild
women of his life

his words are the only
dictionary
and in it i read the poems
i would have written for you

you with the smile his lovers
would have envied

you with the eyes of the
only season

you who stumbled one Sunday evening
on the leftovers of his heart

Cileno

you are the soft hands
of a thousand lovers
in a thousand lifetimes
of poetry written beneath
the giant moons of
those countries built from
pain

your country and mine.

the distance loses itself
in corners of ancient hills
telling their stories
of our grandfathers who fed the earth
their tears. Of their skin, shining
like young olive trees
of the dark, immaculate women who
gave them children and held them
as the sky holds the stars

just beyond the hills
there is your voice
the sound of your guitar
as it bleeds their songs
through your heart.

my tall, Chilean brother
here in the walls of this café

clouded by the smoke of compañeros
by the women who touch you with
quiet smiles
our is the eternal smile
in exile.

The Gift

you will not remember me
after this
i will be another
lifetime away

you will have slept
with one hundred
other women
and will have loved
each one
forever
as you loved me

do not lift your pillow
on nights you lie alone
or you will find
the light from my eyes
will keep you
awake

The Poet

when i was twenty-six
i fell in love with a poet
he was tall and eloquent
and moved like a cloud
on a summer's day
his hands over the keyboard
were magic
and the poems appeared
like miracles
thousands of poems i understood
about the tragedy that
was our immigrant youth
the displacement of our hearts
the tears of our mothers
of young, dead brothers
who lived in photographs
placed lovingly on altars
and on living room walls
the poet made sense of our lives
gave us a place to fit.
he'd move away from the typewriter
satisfied
he'd light the cigarette
and speak to me of the country
that i was
the taste of things Italian

the songs of his grandfather
the ghosts of his past.
i took everything in
like a blessing
secure in my position.
when i was twenty-seven
the poet left
to find other countries
to write about.

Getting Things Right

i am
therefore
i make no apologies
woman
italian
overweight, underweight
tall, loud
romantic bore

i take no responsibility
for his broken heart
his buried body
the vacancies in his life

i accept the colour of my eyes
i will not blame my ancestors
for their darkness
i will not blame them
for my hunger for my desire
to devour the world around me
i am through
blaming the forces outside
my soul
it is unproductive

it is time you stopped
your war with my memory
making me the devil
in your desires
go on, be the priest
you're a great liar.

Sunday and You

take me there, my love
by the brook
beneath the white clouds
knitted in the summer sky

there, by the dry arms
of our tree
where i felt my limbs multiply
and root themselves in you

there, where the jealous sun
watched our eyes fly out
and become poems

and the gentle leaves
embarrassed by our kisses
made a game of our lives

i want to lie by the hem
of the brook with you
eating the sounds
our hearts make

once more

Mother Tells Me Stories

mother tells me stories
of my white cotton dresses
and my long black curls
the days in Ceprano
I held her hand and skipped
all the cobblestones in
Via Alfieri

my sister always wanted ice cream

'do you remember?' she asks
her fingers making ringlets in my hair
I want to scream 'I don't!'

she holds me to her breast
there was a time
by a fireplace
I would not fall asleep
but at her breast

her eyes
are always wet
as she calls me
bimba

For Grandma in Bed, Waiting

your eyes are the wrong colour
there is no darkness in them
to write about
and pain is always dark
your smile comes too easily
pain never smiles
your face contradicts everything
yet, I know your heart is bruised
how can ninety-one years not have bruised
your tiny, fading body
that gave eight children to this world
and scattered thirty grandchildren
like wild flowers in foreign cities.
you have come to end your journey
uncomplaining
in this suburban bungalow
in a room with one window.
you don't always recognize me
but there is something between us
there is the touch of my fingers on
your perfect hand

I come to sit by your bed
not in duty
but in need of the stories
that flow from you

I am in awe, I listen
you take me to your century
I will miss this journey
when you are gone.

The Old Man

a fireplace
an old wooden bench
potatoes buried
under hot ashes
an old man
chews tobacco
and tells stories
of a distant land
he discovered in letters

outside the trees
are furious with the wind

his hands tremble
too many years loving
the wheat in borrowed fields

his eyes are wet moons

too many tall sons
and slenders daughters
have left shadows behind

somewhere in the night
crickets are clowning

and hot ashes are cooling

Il Vecchio

un focolare
un vecchio banco
di legno
patate coperte
da ceneri calde
un vecchio mastica tabacco
e racconta storie
di un paese lontano
scoperto in lettere

fuori gli alberi
sono furiosi col vento

le dita tremano
troppi anni amando il grano
di una terra prestata

i suoi occhi sono lune bagnate

troppi figli
sono ombre lasciate

nella notte
grilli scherzano

e calde ceneri rinfrescano

Dolce-Amaro

he has learned to bend
the way branches do
under the white weight
of endless Januarys.

this country has taken everything
his health, his language
the respect of his modern children
the love of his angry wife.

in some forgotten lifetime
he was a young, dark-haired man
in a ship packed with young
dark-haired men
floating uncomfortably towards
a dream they didn't want to bury
with the still young bones
of mothers and fathers
among the ruins of a postwar Italy.

for most
the dream
did not come easily
the golden paved North America
wasn't paved at all.

there were years of feeling strange
cold and hot months over multiplying bricks

hands turned leathery and large
needs stored away in cave cellars
deep, with the colour of aging wine.

in the evenings
there was the smell of group sweat
cheap meals seasoned with resentment
by the wives of aspiring landlords.

for my father
the dream ended early
when his knees were crushed
by the weight of steel
along some railroad line
he was thirty-one
there was no insurance then
and little interest
for the benefits of the immigrant man.

he bends easily at fifty-seven
walks with a cane
rarely opens his lifeless eyes

the government sends him
fifty-one dollars a month
in recognition.

Novembre 16, 1983

my father is dead
at sixty-one
his heart stopped
his truck stopped
death
at the traffic lights
of Lansdowne and St. Clair

four p.m.
alone
he didn't bother anyone
waited for the red light
so he wouldn't disturb the
traffic.
he was much more considerate
in death
than he had been in life.

my father is dead
and I have nowhere
to put this anger

I was sure he would live
forever
to continue his battle
with me and my
poems.

Tu

mi tocchi
e non ho più fame
sono lì
nei prati
lucciole
margherite e canti
tu
nella distanza
fermo
enormo e sorridente
con le braccia aperte
un olmo
che attende
le mie
mani

Io

io
sono la poesia
l'anello
di matrimonio

io
sono la terra
il peccato
la memoria
la ragione
del loro viaggio

io ancora il respiro
le passioni
sprecate
l'interprete
la lingua straniera
la lingua madre

io
sempre
quella che organizza
il posto
il funerale
le parole
sulla pietra

Sometimes in Teaching

five years of chalk dust in my hair
permanent dandruff
ink spots that will not wash out
on my only silk blouse

five years of Rumpelstiltskin
Rush Cape and Bobby Deerfield
at the lighthouse

five years of fractions
that will not be multiplied

five years of runny noses
bloody knees and hallway vomit.

they've called another staff meeting
we're all going to drown in our
own yawning for the ninety-seventh time

he is going to push a little
christian politics today
'we must learn to sacrifice'
there is little paper
we are out of crayons
only thirty desks per class

where do i put the extra bodies?

and i remember we must sacrifice

Michael knocks
'hiya miss, you need any help?'
he places a sticky lifesaver
in the palm of my hand
'you're the best, miss'

and i know there will
be another five years.

Angelo

Angelo
there is a carnival in town
the wooden horse waits for you
he is frozen
your touch
and the music starts

a thousand wild balloons
are circling the sun
and i want to give you wings
for your seventh birthday

For the Children

for Laura
whose lips are mute
for her eyes
deep in their darkness
for her screams
at story time
the pictures
in her head
the knife, the blood
and her mother's arms
still forever

for Rosa
whose vagina
belonged to her father
for her shuffling feet
her resistance to laughter

for Michael
who is eloquent
with fists
and recoils
from my touch
from any touch

for all their stories
i piece together
for my own child whom i love beyond life

i am here.

Bambini

will you understand
if i speak to you
of the child whose
eyes are melting
like icicles
the one who doesn't
know his name
and six hours
each day he calls me
mother

will you understand
if i speak to you
of the child whose
leg is shorter
than the other
because in that
damn town
buried in distance
they didn't understand
disease

will you understand
if i speak to you
of the child
whose body is
mapped by belt buckles

because she is the
fifth girl to be born
to an immigrant
father

will you understand
the child
whose only toy
is a human
brother?

For My Uncle

I have heard
you have two sons
secret sons
twins
tall, handsome boys
professionals
born in 1948
when you left
town
and them
for the American dream

1980
and your dreams
hang over a hospital bed
in a plastic bag
with white liquid

this new wife
with the olympic tongue
holding your hand
and me
the poet niece
who tells jokes
to watch your smile
your hands are still beautiful
unaffected by forty years of

Canadian life
the long thin fingers
have resisted well
they tap the fading blanket
for hours
resisting
still.

The Red Scooter

Filomena's mother died today
the phone call in the middle
of the night
they can never seem to figure out
the difference in time from here
to Italy.

when i remember Filomena
i feel a burning in my eyes
the envy in my heart
for her big brick house
like a mansion on a hill
in Via Santa Maria
the garden of giant zinnias
blood red roses
the locked, iron gate.

each morning her father
the Blackshirt *maresciallo*
would take her to school
on his bright red vespa scooter
they would pass me by and wave
her long, thick hair flapping away.
their laughter hung in the wind
long after they had disappeared
over the bridge of the Fiume Liri.
how i envied her little red scooter

and her big, tall father with
his arms around her.

my steps over the stones
patiently walking to school
dreaming of my father in Canada
waiting for me in his big, red
Cadillac.

his hand
suspended in the air
like a great, weightless cloud
it came down across her face
and she fell to the ground.
he stood over her
anger and hate in his eyes
her frightened arms
absorbing the blows
while her screams
like bullets
punctured the countryside
his hands became fists
hammering
like thunder
her body, her hair
her arms became one.
and then silence.
his shadow over her
was a great mountain
a thousand eyes watched
paralysed
and with one long breath
he moved away
leaving her
to the attending
vultures.

Nina, la matta

the neighbours think she's crazy
running out in the middle of the night
in her underwear
to hide in the garage
like a wounded animal
hungry
for warmth and safety.

they think her screams
are of a woman gone mad
with superstition.

she pours bags of salt
on the green grass around her house
to keep away the evil eye
there are crosses and beads
everywhere
knives in plastic bags
buried beneath her veranda.

the neighbours know nothing
of the jagged glass
he tried to shove into her vagina
as their six-year-old son watched
they know nothing of her beaten body
hurled down cellar stairs
like discarded work shoes.

she walks to church each day
talking to the air
plastic flowers for the Madonna
she touches the blue marble gown
and then her lips.
on her knees she walks the length
of the church for hours
everyone thinks she's mad.

Marisa

Marisa
si piega
verso i figli
si piega
verso il marito
si piega
verso tutto

Marisa
si volta
dallo specchio
non considera
la faccia
non riconosce
i suoi occhi

Marisa
ride dolcemente
mentre scansa
i suoi
sogni
nascondendo nei cassetti
pezzetti del suo
cuore.

Success

you have grown fat
with your husband's success

never asking more
than was needed
for the children
for the freezer
that kept half a cow
perfectly cool

now your own child
is making babies
your husband
is measuring
his masculinity
with firmer breasts

and you sit, undisturbed
on all the blue silks
surrounding the
cold breath of
your saints.

Mary

I

Mary jumped
from stone to stone
small islands shining
in the August sun

she lost her balance
the water kissed her knees

I watched her
and loved her
the closest thing to an Angel

she came to me
smiled her Angel smile
our fingers touching
we walked home.

II

well, little sister
it is the second year
of your new state
the woman
the wife
two years since you

dropped your laughter
in the music box
on the dresser
and walked out, smiling
in your white dress
with the thousand pearls
you left a shadow in our
bedroom that never sleeps
tonight
I will stay in another room.

III

our bodies were foreign countries
never to be looked at
never to be touched
never to be understood
preserved in plastic
like Teresa's couch and chair
like her giardiniera
petrified in vinegar
to last forever
for some great, sacred
feast.

Mary's breasts drip with
acid milk
she cannot feed her child
it will not nourish
it will not fill.

her eyes are deep, dark
question marks
she cannot control the hormones
going wild inside her veins
her tortured cries.

my arms around her like a prayer
to flush out this devil
we do not understand
our hands bonded, like children
I am here, please heal.

IV

she believes she's going crazy
but she doesn't know why
exploring the reasons
with each bead at
her fingertips.

her life is perfect
she believes in God
and her husband

she adores the children
her home is comfortable
except she hates the kitchen

sitting by the light of the porch
staring into the dim suburban stars
the tears find their way into her lap
like large, clear stones.

perhaps tomorrow she will smile
the pills will work
tomorrow.

V

suburban grass is perfect
in a year my new nephew
will plant his knees everywhere
he will be green
like the neighbourhood.

suburban flowers are neat
and quiet, they remind me
of my grandmother's hands
at the end.

Mary sits
in the tall, brittle shade
on her dried flowers
in her white living room
Van Gogh colours in her
eyes.

I visit often   —
to hold my new nephew
and to reminisce
of the days when we were
nieces
and all the living rooms
were open spaces.

Compleanno

i want to eat a ripe fig
i want to steal a persimmon
from old Alfredo's trees
have him catch me in the act
watching him stumble over the pitchfork
as he tries to grab me
my mouth smeared orange
from the sweet flesh of
the forbidden fruit.
i want to hide behind the
mountains of dry hay
feeling the cool breath of
autumn's lungs.
I want to climb the chestnut tree
and guard the rooftops over the
countryside, listening to the
soft voices singing Roman songs.
i want to run my hands through
the rosemary bush by the gate
where my grandmother's iris grows
to sit by the stone wall
waiting for mamma
as she pedals back from town
on her old, black bike
her pockets full of chocolates
and then to sleep

in linen sheets
warmed by hot bricks
wrapped in flannel
to dream of ripe purple figs
on freshly baked bread.

Beautiful Things

brave, beautiful things
have their own shape
the belly at nine months
the winter maple in my backyard
in its January coat
the light above the photograph
of Gia at three months
they do not need words they are.

the cemetery where my father
sleeps in winter, spring
forever.

i walk down the perfect stone path
to the tall mausoleum
placing flowers by his name
he lies on the sixth floor
overlooking the stillness
the numbness of peace.

these flowers will breathe
the ice of his month
and they will be beautiful
in silence.

i come, i sit
i visit with this man
i could never talk to
and have long conversations.

First Snow

i imagine this is the silence
of a soul at peace
three a.m.
the first snow of this winter
it is pure
it is wanted
the bare branches of my cherry tree
are crisp fingers of ice
they shimmer by the light of the school yard
there are no footsteps to interrupt
this perfection
i sit and smoke my cigarette, slowly
and let my eyes feast
while my husband and child
sleep in the heart of their down quilts
this moment is mine
alone with thoughts that smile
in my head
the coming of Christmas
it is my favourite time
the joy of family at its best
the celebration of love
of this one Canadian thing
i crave
the beauty and silence of the
first snow

Easter-Resurrection

for Delia

when your friends die in their forties
you mourn the loss of them
you mourn the loss of yourself.
it is not supposed to happen in your forties
there is a numbness that defies explanation
it is the fear of leaving
unannounced, unprepared
and nothing is in order
the photographs in drawers
the laundry still in the bins
and your child
who will be there
for her communion
her wedding
and the history you must provide

i hear my heart beating
in the bone of sleepless nights
thinking of you
gone, disappeared
plastered into a structure
in a Protestant cemetery
no more seasons.

the Easter lilies are out
i will bring one to you
with the prayers we learned
in our lifetime
this resurrection our priest
talks about
it still eludes me.

Grace Street Summer

the moon is almost round tonight
a plane just flew over it
like a cartoon
it is lifting over Tony's garage
ripe as a honeydew melon
my thumb stretched out
we play hide-and-seek.
the schoolyard is loud
with boys and basketballs
in the distance Benny's radio
tuned to C.H.I.N. and calabrian songs
his wife's voice in harmony
her doughy, round body
by the kitchen window
floating from sink to cupboard
dishes and cutlery being put to bed.
my daughter and her best friend Bianca
skipping to silly schoolgirl rhymes
i'm under the cherry tree
swollen ankles propped
on the little brick wall
soon Andrew will bring out espresso
with a touch of grappa
good for the digestion
we will talk into the night
wanting summer to last forever.

i want to remember this
next time i'm angry at life.

For Gia at Bedtime

she smells of something so beautiful
it has no name
her face is the passion fruit flower
i held in my hands as a child
and never let go
she brings back all the evenings
of spring in the farmhouse
she gives her smile freely
without conditions
she loves the size of my belly.
i read her stories
in her room of painted giraffes and clouds
she does not interrupt
i watch her stretch her long, thin arm
over her favourite blanket
and close her eyes.

i think of poems i might write
but there is no image
for this moment
for who she is
my only daughter
my prayer
the greatest poem of my life.

Gianna Patriarca was born in Ceprano, Frosinone, in the region of Lazio. She came to Canada in 1960 with her mother and sister to join her father who had emigrated in 1956. For the past thirty years she has lived, studied and worked in the city of Toronto.

She received a B.A. and B.Ed. from York University and is presently teaching for the Metro Separate School Board.

***

Some of her poems have appeared in *Jewish Dialogue, Fireweed: A Woman's Journal, L'Étranger* (anthology), *Poetry Toronto Newsletter, Poetry Canada Review, The Worker, Quaderni Canadesi* and *Il Laghetto*.

• Cap-Saint-Ignace
• Sainte-Marie (Beauce)
Québec, Canada
1996